World Religions General Editor: Raymond F. Trudgian

UNDERSTANDING YOUR HINDU NEIGHBOUR

JOHN EWAN

Senior Lecturer in Religious Studies
Preston Polytechnic

LUTTERWORTH EDUCATIONAL
GUILDFORD, SURREY

First published 1977
Reprinted 1983

ISBN 0 7188 1800 8

COPYRIGHT © 1977 JOHN EWAN

Printed in Great Britain by
Fletcher & Son Ltd, Norwich

CONTENTS

LIST OF ILLUSTRATIONS

The author and publishers wish to express their gratitude to the Camera Press, London, for permission to reproduce illustrations no. 4 (by A. Gregory), 2 and 15 (by R. J. Chinwalla); and to Ram Bhakta of Loughborough for permission to reproduce a photograph (no. 12) of his painting.

The author further wishes to thank members of the Hindu community in Preston for their kindness and hospitality and the information so readily given, especially Mr. V. G. Patel and his family, and Mr. G. Patel, President and Secretary respectively of the Gujarati Hindu Society in Preston.

EDITOR'S INTRODUCTION

The response to our *Thinking About* series showed the need for basic foundation books which could be used by pupils in Junior and Middle Schools. The books in this *Understanding Your Neighbour* series present the festivals, places of worship and other customs of the various faiths now represented in this country.

The children who use these books will have reached what Jean Piaget, the educational psychologist, calls the 'concrete' stage of thinking. This is defined in *Religious Education in Primary Schools* (Schools Council Working Paper 44) as the stage where, 'the child now begins to be able to think more logically, to relate different aspects of a situation, to classify data, and to check over his thinking. He is still limited, however, to thinking mainly about specific objects . . .'

This research has been borne in mind in the preparation of these books. It is now becoming accepted that World Religions can be dealt with at the Junior and Middle School level by introducing the specific festivals and customs of other people. Another accepted approach is through the use of themes such as 'light' and 'water', elements known to the pupil which recur in the practices of many religions.

The General Article introducing the Christian Education Movement Primary Resource material on 'Living in a Multi-Faith Society' agrees that this phenomenological approach is the way to study other faiths in the classroom but states that this method, 'Can easily degenerate into a "bits and pieces" method'. It goes on to say:

> Most religious beliefs and practices can be understood only in the context of the faith as a whole, and great care must be taken therefore to select only those examples which are not misleading when studied apart from that context . . . While pupils cannot be expected to see religion as a whole, teachers should not venture into the field of other faiths without the support of good resource material and without the willingness to study the religion seriously and gain some sort of overall understanding.

We have attempted to present this 'overall' picture in these books in such a way that not only the teacher but also the pupil can come to a balanced understanding of their neighbours' faith.

The specific and concrete examples of events, customs and buildings are presented in the context of the faith in order to help the pupil not only to acquire new facts but to perceive the experience of a child who lives in another culture.

Through the study of this series of books, pupils should be able to discover their own themes and to see the similarities and differences.

Again to quote from the CEM Primary Resource material:

> World Religions in Education is certainly not an attempt to gloss over differences, to pretend that all religions are really the same, but it does help pupils to see that the religious quest is common to mankind, that certain elements are found in most religions, e.g. worship, sacred places, sacred writing, beliefs about the significance of a man, a sense of the mystery of life, etc. even if the form may vary. The emphasis is on what unites men rather than on what divides them.

This is the emphasis of these books as they seek to lay a foundation of knowledge and appreciation in the Primary school to counteract the stereotype so prevalent in their environment which often prevents them from 'Understanding their Neighbour'.

Isleworth, Middlesex   Raymond F. Trudgian

AUTHOR'S INTRODUCTION

In this book we shall be introduced to a family of Hindus from the state of Gujarat in the west of India who have settled in Britain. Some of the customs of Hindus from other parts of India may differ from what is described here but, because a large number of Hindus in Britain are from Gujarat, we shall be looking at the life of a Gujarati family and the community in which they live.

We shall visit their home and share a meal with them, join them as they worship God in their temple, and enjoy the great variety of festivals which they celebrate each year. We shall also learn about the ceremonies performed at birth, marriage and death.

The Patel family, to whom we shall be introduced, is not a real one, but there are many families like them who would welcome you to their community centres, their temples and their homes.

A NOTE TO TEACHER'S

It would be advantageous to use a book of Hindu tales and legends to supplement the material in this book. The following are recommended for such use:

Cradle Tales of Hinduism by Sister Nivedita (Ramakrishna Vedanta Centre, London);
One Man and his Dog by Henry Lefever (Lutterworth Press);
The Legends of Lord Ganesha by S. Bhoothalingam (India Book House Education Trust).

For further information on Hinduism, its teaching in schools, and useful lists of books and other resources teachers may refer to:

Hinduism by J. R. Hinnells and E. J. Sharpe (Oriel Press);
World Religions: Aids for Teachers (Community Relations Commission);
Thinking About Hinduism by Eric J. Sharpe (Lutterworth Press).

THE PATEL FAMILY

The Patel family comes from a village near Surat in the state of Gujarat, about 150 miles north of the city of Bombay in India.

They have been in Britain for ten months, having arrived in November just in time for the cold, wet months of the year, and are now preparing for their second winter.

These are the names of the members of the family:

Shri (Mr.) *Prakash Patel*: called by his family *Baba* or *Papa* (which means Daddy).

Shrimati (Mrs.) *Saraswati Patel*: called by the family *Ba* or simply Mummy.

Kamala is their elder daughter and she is nineteen years old; plans for her marriage are already well under way.

Krishna is their only son, eleven years old.

Sumitra is their younger daughter, also eleven years old.

The two youngest, the twins Krishna and Sumitra, are just about to start their first term at Secondary school.

Mr. Patel's mother and father have recently come from Gujarat to live with the family. They are called:

Bharat: known to the family as *Dadaji* (which means Grandpa).

Parvati: known to the family as *Ma* or as *Dadima* (which means Grandma).

A number of their relatives are living in different parts of Britain; Mr. Patel's brother lives in the Midlands, and comes to visit them from time to time. His name is *Ramdas* and he is known as *Kaka* (which means Uncle).

1. A Hindu family at home.

FIRST TERM AT SECONDARY SCHOOL

The long summer holidays had come to an end. At Brockbank High School the children were arriving for the first day of the new school year.

Many of them were with friends from their junior schools, but some had fairly recently arrived from overseas, from India, Pakistan and Bangladesh, from the Caribbean, Cyprus and even China; for them the school seemed rather strange. For all the children, of course, it was a new experience, and made them feel a bit nervous, although they didn't want others to notice it.

Errol was from Jamaica; he had been at the local junior school for two years; Muhammad from Pakistan already had an elder brother at the school.

Krishna and Sumitra had hardly settled into their junior school before the time came to move on to secondary school; so they naturally felt rather lost at first. They still found it difficult to make themselves understood in English; Sumitra especially was worried that she would not be able to understand what the teachers were saying, and so would fall behind the rest of the class in her work. But she need not have been so worried, for

2. *Raksha Bandhan*, the tie of friendship and protection.

some older pupils were detailed to take them to their classroom and explain to them what they had to do.

Their class teacher soon put them at ease by asking them their names and where they all came from, as he marked the register. He talked about some of the names, and wrote them on the blackboard; he seemed to know a great deal about them.

Here is a list of a few Indian and English first names whose meanings are similar.

Indian names		*English names*	
Deepak	= Light or Lamp	Helen	= Light
Shanti	= Peace	Irene	= Peace
Kamala	= Lotus-eyed	Susan	= Lily or Lotus
Raja	= King	Basil	= King
Charulata	= Beautiful gift from God	Jane	= Gift from God
Saraswati	= a Hindu goddess	Diana	= a Roman goddess
Narendra	= a Prince	Sarah	= a Princess

Sumitra was surprised to hear that her elder sister's name, Kamala, had the same meaning as Susan; and the girl who sat next to her in class was called Susan. She would remember to tell Kamala that.

13

For the first few days Krishna and Sumitra walked about on their own at break-times. Krishna had promised to look after his sister until they had settled into the new school. In fact Sumitra had been worried about going to secondary school, and had asked him to do so at a family festival in the summer holidays.

This festival is called *Raksha Bandhan* (*Raksha* means protection and *Bandhan* means a tie). It is a traditional ceremony dating from the days of chivalry. The girl ties threads or a star round the wrists of the brother, cousin or family friend whom she has chosen, and he promises to come to her aid if she needs it. Of course, there is often plenty of laughter and teasing, but the boy is expected to keep his promise.

In the playground most of the children kept to their own groups, but one day Susan Clarke, the girl who sat next to her in class, asked Sumitra to join in a game of hopscotch with her. She had been longing to ask if she could play, because it was a game they played in India. She told Susan that they called it *Langadi* or sometimes *Ikki dukki*, and marked the squares out with chalk, drawing the Indian numbers in the squares.

This is what it looked like:

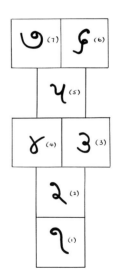

3. Hopscotch—Indian style.

Susan's brother Peter got talking to Krishna, and it was not long before Peter and some others were explaining how to play conkers and marbles and teaching him to play French cricket; Krishna too had summoned up enough confidence to explain to them the rules of a game they used to play at home in India, which he called *Gilli danda*. The rules of the game

14

vary from one part of India to another, but it is played more or less like this:

The *Gilli* is a small round piece of stick, about 10 cm long, tapered to a point at both ends, and is used as a ball.
The *Danda* is a longer and thicker stick, about 45 cm in length, and is used as a bat.
The player taps the *Gilli* with the *Danda* to make it jump up, then tries to hit it as far as he can.
If a member of the fielding team catches the *Gilli*, the player who hit it is out; if it is not caught, he scores points according to how far he has hit it. The team with the most points.wins.

Peter was very surprised to discover, when he told his family about it that evening, that a similar game (called Pig and Stick) was one of the games his father had played when he was at school in Yorkshire.

Krishna and Sumitra soon settled down to the routine of school life; they soon spoke English fluently thanks to their friendship with the Clarkes, and as their English improved, so did their position in the class; Krishna was even third in the class in mathematics.

As their parents were both out at work all day, they had to stay for school dinners and, in common with many others, did not like them very much, mainly because the food was rather different from what they were used to at home. There was usually some choice of menu, but there was some difficulty one day, when the only dish being served included beef. Krishna asked if they could have something different. They were given cheese salad but, all the same, they felt as if everyone was looking at them.

Peter was curious to know why they didn't eat beef. Sumitra explained that they were Hindus, and their religion did not allow them to eat it, just as the Muslims could not eat pork. She said that in India cows were very special animals and had to be treated with great respect. It was a crime to kill cows, which were allowed to wander through the streets, helping themselves to whatever they wanted from the shops; no one would try to stop them.

Sumitra couldn't find the words to explain why the cow was so special, but she did remember that once a year in October there was a festival day in honour of cows. On that day their cow (for they had had a cow of their own when they lived in Gujarat) was washed and brushed till her coat gleamed, her horns were decorated with garlands of flowers, and she was given an extra supply of hay before being led in procession with other cows along the village street.

4. Sacred cows in an Indian street.

The first-years were beginning to study a second language — French — and were discussing with their teacher the many languages of the world. Peter was amazed to hear that Krishna's family could already speak three languages: Gujarati, their mother tongue which they usually spoke at home; Hindi, the official language used by the government in India; and now English, for their education at school. He was beginning to wonder whether he would ever manage even two languages himself! At break-time one day Krishna showed Peter his own name, and Sumitra's, in the Gujarati script.

This is what the script looked like:

KRISHNA   SUMITRA

5. The Gujarati script.   કૃષ્ણ   સુમિત્ર

Peter was surprised to see that whereas the English letters sit on the line, the Gujarati letters hang under the line.

16

In their English lessons they were reading stories and legends from different parts of the world, and were being encouraged to write down their favourite stories in their books. Sumitra's special favourite was the story of Rama and Sita, in which Vishnu the great God and Lakshmi his wife came down to earth in the form of Rama and Sita, because they felt that was the only way to help mankind to defeat the demons who were creating havoc in the world. This is one of the best known stories in India. Sumitra had been taught to follow the good examples of Rama and Sita in all she did, and she could still remember the time when Ma had first told her the story, as they sat by the fire at home on a winter evening, when she was about four years old.

The English teacher was pleased with Sumitra's story, which she found very interesting; in fact both Krishna and Sumitra were now thoroughly settled at school and had 'made good progress', as their school report said. Their parents were pleased, as they were most anxious that they should succeed at school.

A few of the children didn't attend assembly, or stay in the religious education lessons, but the Patels, like most Hindus, were quite happy for their children to take part in these activities. They considered religion to be very important, and taught their own children about it at home and at the temple. So Krishna and Sumitra went to the school assemblies and enjoyed them. Their parents saw no reason why they should not learn about other religions; after all, as far as they could see most religious people really believed in the same God, although they might have different ways of describing him and worshipping him.

There was one thing which troubled Sumitra. Their class had physical education lessons once a week, and in their second term they were to go to the swimming baths. At the junior school she had been able to join in everything, including P.E., but she knew that her mother was not anxious to let her change into shorts and T-shirt, or to go to swimming lessons. In India it was the custom for girls of secondary school age to keep their arms and legs covered, and not to mix with boys.

Sumitra had told her mother that boys and girls had P.E. lessons separately; she wasn't sure whether she would be allowed to join in, but she hoped it would be possible. In the end Mr. Patel sent a note to the school explaining their problem, and Sumitra and a few other girls were allowed to wear tracksuits in the P.E. lessons. She was also allowed to go swimming, as the boys and girls went on separate days. Some of her friends were not allowed to go at all, so Sumitra was very thankful that her parents had raised no objection.

17

On their way home from school Krishna and Sumitra walked past the house where Peter and Susan lived. One day they were asked to stay and play after school. The next day, with their father's permission, they went home with their friends. It was the first time that Krishna and Sumitra had been in a British home, and they thoroughly enjoyed themselves.

It wasn't long before the two families met while out walking in the park on a Saturday afternoon. They all walked together, chatting as they went, and Mr. Patel invited all the Clarke family to a meal the following Saturday evening.

They were very pleased to be invited, of course, but a little nervous, as they didn't know what to expect.

AT HOME WITH THE PATELS

The Clarkes were given a great welcome when they arrived. Mr. Patel met them at the door, saying *Namaskaras* (which means 'Greetings') bowing slightly as he did so, and placing his hands together in front of him; then, to make them feel more at home, he shook hands with them all.

It is most important for Hindus to show hospitality at all times; in fact in one of the Hindu scriptures it is said that 'guests are gods', especially unexpected or uninvited guests. This means that the Hindu can go to his friends or relatives at any time, even in the middle of the night, and still be made welcome, for the host should always show the same respect for guests as he does for God.

It took a while for everyone to be introduced. Apart from Krishna and Sumitra, there was Kaka (Uncle) Ramdas, Mr. Patel's brother, on a visit from his home in the Midlands; Kamala, their elder sister, who was nineteen years old and to be married in the spring; and Dadaji (Grandpa) and Ma (Grandma), Mr. Patel's parents, who had only arrived in August from Gujarat to join the family, and remained silent in the background, unable as yet to speak much English.

Mrs. Patel was nowhere to be seen, but the sounds and smells coming from the kitchen told their own story; the meal was nearly ready. Before they sat down around the table, they all washed their hands with great care under a running tap in the kitchen. As Mrs. Patel brought in the food, she told them what everything was called: a vegetable curry, lentils with boiled rice, and papadums which were rather like very tasty crisps. Each person had several bowls and dishes; the rice was placed on the main dish,

18

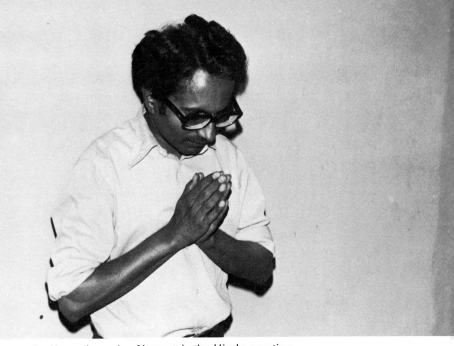

6. *Namaskaras* (or *Namaste*), the Hindu greeting.

Namaskaras is the traditional Hindu greeting. It simply means 'showing respect'. Both hands are joined together, fingers to fingers, palms to palms, and usually raised to the level of the chest to greet your equals, to the forehead or above to greet especially important people or when you are praying to a god. The hands are held in such a position that they join together the chest, head and arms, so to speak, thus showing that you respect the person with your heart, mind and strength. The hands are often held in this position too when asking for something or thanking someone. Hindus do not often thank people in words: this does not mean they are ungrateful, simply that they believe real gratitude to be shown more by what you do than by what you say.

the lentils, called *dal*, were in a small bowl, some carrots and 'ladyfingers' in another dish, green chillies, and very tasty hot lemon chutney.

Before they began to eat Mr. Patel sprinkled a little water over the food and silently asked God to bless it. There was a small bowl of water for them to rinse their fingers when they became sticky. Knives, forks and spoons were provided, but they were all invited to eat with their fingers. After some hesitation they decided to give it a try, and with some help from a spoon from time to time they managed very well. It wasn't such a messy business after all, but as Mr. Clarke said, it required a technique just as using a knife and fork did. Krishna said that he had felt quite scared of using cutlery when they had first stayed to dinner at their primary school, and he understood how difficult it must be for them to eat sticky food with their fingers for the first time. Mr. Patel explained that only the right hand was used for eating; the left hand was used for toilet and for dirty tasks. When washing you had to be sure that the right hand was especially clean. It was often difficult to tell if cutlery was really clean, but at least you made quite sure that your own hand was clean.

Each of them had been provided with a glass of water; Susan was thankful for that, because, although the curry had been quite mild, she had tried some hot chillies without realizing what they were; but with the water and a small bowl of *dahi* (yoghurt) she soon cooled down. When they had all finished, and washed and dried their hands, they sat by the fire to talk, and some *vayiari* was handed round. This consisted of a fine mixture of seeds, and was used as an aid to digestion.

All this time Mrs. Patel and Ma had busied themselves making sure that the guests and her family were well fed, and only now did they have some food themselves. Mrs. Patel said that this was the custom, and she never ate till her husband and Dadaji had first eaten. As Mr. Patel was the head of the household, he did most of the talking, though it was Kaka Ramdas who answered when Mr. Clarke asked if they were vegetarians. He said that, like many Hindus, they didn't eat meat at all at home, but they didn't mind eating meat when they were away from home, if there were nothing else available. The one thing they would not eat under any circumstances was beef. He explained that the cow had been considered sacred for more than two thousand years in India. She was more than a pet, she was the most important and useful animal a villager could possess. She gave milk, provided for their needs, and nourished them like a mother. She was gentle and harmless, a constant companion of man.

Once long ago, he said, when demons had brought destruction upon the world, the god Vishnu chose to come down to earth in the form of a cowherd in order to bring peace and prosperity to men once again. Many are the stories of this cowherd, Krishna, and his exploits. So the cow is always very well looked after, and treated as a member of the family. They would rather go hungry themselves than let a cow starve. To harm a cow is as serious a crime as to hurt your own mother. This respect for the cow, he said, helped the Hindu to remember to be kind and considerate to all living beings, animals and plants as well as humans, for in them all there is part of the spirit of God. (Hindus have a special word for this respect for life, *ahimsa*, usually called 'non-violence'.)

Talking of Krishna, the cowherd, reminded Mr. Patel of the recently

20

7. A Hindu temple, the Shri Geeta Bhawan Mandir, in Birmingham.

opened Hindu Centre and its Prayer Hall. It had been opened at a special ceremony in the summer holiday, and they were all very proud of it.

He was most anxious to show them round it as soon as possible, and before they said good-bye they arranged a time to go down to the Hindu Centre together.

THE HINDU CENTRE

One evening, when their parents were back from work, they all went down to the new Hindu Centre. It was in an old primary school. In the summer it had been officially opened by a *pandit* (a learned man) who had come from Gujarat to install the statues of Krishna and Radha in the Prayer Hall. Appropriately enough, the opening ceremony was held on the very day of the festival of *Janam Ashtami* (the birthday of Lord Krishna).

Mr. Patel said that, although some had wanted to call the Centre a Temple, they had eventually agreed to call it the 'Hindu Cultural and Recreational Centre', because they wanted it to be a place where people could not only meet for worship but also attend language classes, come to sports evenings, or enjoy making music and dancing; and, of course, it would be an ideal place for families to hold their wedding ceremonies.

While the grown-ups were talking about these things, the children were exploring the back of the building; Krishna took them round the library, the kitchens, the games room, and then out into the large yard where they often played when their family came down to the Centre in the evenings. Some of the rooms were still not completely decorated, and Krishna and Peter had already privately agreed to help clear the rooms one evening.

The children re-joined their parents in the main hall. The week before they had held their first big meeting there, when the pandit had talked to the people about their religion. The hall had been packed that day; there was a carpet so that the audience could all sit comfortably on the floor. At one end was a platform, on which was a rolled-up mattress and a large cushion. The speaker always sat cross-legged on the mattress as he talked to the people.

The Prayer Hall

It was nearly seven o'clock and quite a few people were making their way into the Prayer Hall, so they all went in together to join the worship. Before they entered, like everyone else, they took off their shoes as a sign of respect. They found themselves in a large hall, where a warm, comfortable carpet covered the floor from wall to wall; the ceiling and the walls were decorated with colourful designs and large, framed pictures of the Hindu gods; there was a frieze, which stretched all round the hall, telling the story of Lord Krishna's life.

All this they took in at a glance, but Mr. Patel had now paused by a small niche in the wall. In it stood a marble statue of Ganesha, the elephant-headed god; no one went in without first paying their respects to him, and asking him to help them in their worship. Mrs. Patel gave Sumitra a flower to place beside Ganesha. Susan noticed another niche on the other side of the hall; in it was a statue of Hanuman, the monkey general. Susan remembered that it was Hanuman who had helped Rama in his struggle against the wicked Ravana, the story which she had heard at school.

Now that they were well inside the hall, they noticed that there were several small groups of people sitting cross-legged on the carpet, waiting for the evening worship to begin. They were saying their *japam*, that is, repeating the names of God. They might spend a long time simply repeating over and over again a holy word or phrase, like *Om jai Jagdish Hare* which means, 'Victory to thee, O God, Lord of the universe'. This helps them to forget themselves and all their daily worries, and to concentrate on the worship of God.

22

8. Evening prayers at the Hindu Centre, Preston.

9. A shrine to Lord Krishna and Radha.

At one end of the hall, raised on a dais and under a brightly lit canopy, were the statues — almost life-size — of Lord Krishna playing his flute, and Radha his companion. This was the main shrine, where everyone came to worship. On the steps of the shrine was a tray containing incense sticks, a bowl of holy water and a lamp-holder.

All the Patel family, beginning with Mr. Patel, moved to the front, standing at the bottom of the steps before Lord Krishna and Radha. He bowed in reverence, hands held together in *namaskaras*; he said his own prayers and offered *prasad*, (which means a gift), which consisted in his case of a few grains of rice and some money which he placed in the box provided. By this time, as many people had arrived for worship, there was quite a pile of gifts, of apples, coconuts and sweets, and the money-box sounded full. Mrs. Patel and the children followed his example. Then they all sat down with the rest of the people, and were joined by the Clarkes.

While the priest was preparing for the service, Sumitra was pointing things out to Susan. The statues of Krishna and Radha were dressed in blue clothes, and Sumitra proudly told her that she had helped her mother to make them. There was a different set of clothes for every day of the year, and they were all in slightly different designs, even if many of them had to be the same colour.

24

10. The priest conducts the evening *Arti* — the Hindu Centre, Preston.

The gifts were all neatly laid on trays in front of the shrine, the curtains were drawn across the front of the statues, and the people joined in a prayer asking God to come down and accept the gifts which they had offered to him.

Now it was *Arti* time, the most important part of the worship. The curtains were drawn back, and everyone stood up to praise God, thanking him for accepting their worship. The priest lifted the lamp-holder, with its many flames flickering, and swung it from side to side in front of the shrine, ringing a bell loudly as he did so. One of the boys was given the conch-shell, which he blew for as long as he was able while the people chanted the prayers. The priest then moved down the steps of the shrine, and went through the same motions in front of the statues of Ganesha, Hanuman and Ambaji the Divine Mother.

Returning to the shrine, he took some water (which was holy water from the sacred river Ganges in North India) and scattered it over the worshippers. The drummers began to beat out a rhythm, and the people clapped their hands as they sang a hymn to Lord Krishna.

A girl of about Sumitra's age brought the lamp-holder round to the people, who put small coins on the tray and held their hands over the flames before passing them over their faces, as if to receive the power of God into

25

their hearts. Then bowls of holy Ganges water, and of milk, were taken round, and each person held out the right hand to taste just a little of each. One of the younger children distributed napkins to everyone, and some older girls handed out the *prasad*, a mixture of nuts, dried fruit, banana and sugar crystals.

The priest concluded by reading a chapter from the *Gita*, one of the holy scriptures, and explaining it to them; the worship ended with the repeating of the names of God, and the words *Om, Shanti, Shanti, Shanti* (which means 'O God, Peace, Peace, Peace').

To Peter and Susan, in fact to all the Clarkes, this was a completely new experience, and they had many questions to ask. 'Why,' said Peter, 'do you bring these gifts, and what happens to the food which is left over?' Mr. Patel answered, 'The gifts are to give thanks for all the good things of life which God gives us; the food which is left over will be used later for meals which are provided for guests who come to the Centre'.

Mrs. Clarke wanted to know if they had a copy of their holy scriptures, like the Holy Bible kept in Christian churches on a lectern. In answer they were taken to a table beside the shrine, and shown a very large and extremely heavy book, which had to be taken out of a glass case. When the silk cover had been untied, and the book opened, they saw that it was beautifully printed in black script with red decoration. It was a copy of the four parts of the *Veda*, the oldest and most holy of all the Hindu writings. (*Veda* means 'knowledge'.)

Susan was quick to notice that it was written in a different script from the Gujarati they had seen elsewhere. Mr. Patel told them that, although he could read it, he could not understand it very well, as it was in the ancient language of Sanskrit. There was an inscription in Sanskrit up on the wall beside the shrine, so he read it out to them: 'The Lord Krishna is my refuge'.

Mr. Patel himself read the Gita, often in an English translation, which was much easier to understand. The pandits and priests were experts in the Vedas, but they were not often able to come; one day they hoped to employ a priest full-time who would live at the Centre, look after the shrine and teach the people. In addition, he would be able to conduct the important religious ceremonies like the name-giving, the Sacred Thread ceremony, and the wedding and funeral rites.

The priests belonged to the Brahmin caste, the highest caste in India, and only they could perform religious ceremonies in the proper way. In India people have for centuries been divided into four main classes, which are known as castes: the Brahmins (priests); the Kshatriyas (rulers and

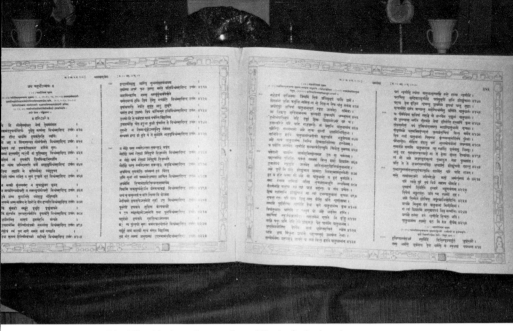

11. The Vedas, the ancient Hindu holy book.

soldiers); the Vaishyas (businessmen and farmers); and the Shudras (manual workers). The Patels belonged to the Vaishya class of businessmen. In Britain caste is no longer so important, but it is usual for Hindus to associate with people of their own caste, and for most Hindus it is still essential that marriages should be between people of the same caste.

Time was slipping by; there were many more questions in their minds. Peter wanted to know all about Lord Krishna, but that would have to wait. Before they went Sumitra was sent by her mother to fetch some more prasad. They were each given two small bags: one of them was full of *ganchia* which consisted of sticks and curls of flour and spices which had been fried; the other contained *bundi*, a sticky sweet mixture. Then Mr. Patel said good-bye to them, saying that he hoped they would come to the Centre whenever they liked. They would always be very welcome.

GRANDMA THE STORYTELLER

Often in the Patel household, after the meal was over and the younger children were getting ready for bed, Ma would sit with them and tell them the old stories she had learnt from her mother long ago. Krishna could still remember, when they lived in Gujarat, sitting beside Ma on the veranda in the cool of the evening as the moon rose higher in the sky, looking out into the courtyard and listening to the tales of Lord Krishna and his pranks as a child. It wasn't the same in Britain; it was often too cold to sit outside, and television programmes seemed to have taken the place of storytelling. However, this was one of the evenings when the television was silent and they sat quietly while Ma told the old familiar stories which she knew so well that she could almost have told them in her sleep.

One was the story of Lord Krishna, which told how, when evil threatened to upset the balance of the world, the god Vishnu came to earth in human form to overcome the evil and teach men to live peaceably with one another. To this day Hindus celebrate the birthday of Lord Krishna (*Janam Ashtami*) and remember the times when the cowherds and milkmaids danced to the music of Krishna's flute at Brindaban at the spring festival of Holi (see pages 49–50).

Peter and Susan went to play at the Patels' quite often. In their hall and in their kitchen hung brightly coloured pictures of the elephant-headed god which they had seen at the entrance to the Prayer Hall at the Centre. There were pictures of other gods and goddesses as well, but Ganesha seemed different from the rest; in fact, both of them thought he was rather odd and very ugly, and asked their friends why they worshipped a god like that.

Krishna said that, as it happened, only a week before they had celebrated *Ganesha Chaturthi* (the festival of Ganesha). Ganesha is one of the children's favourite gods; all over India and especially in Maharashtra (part of Western India) the festival is celebrated with great enthusiasm. Clay models of Ganesha are made and worshipped at home for a day or two, then they are taken out in a procession, and finally submerged in the river or the 'tank' (the village pond) where they quickly disintegrate.

Here in Britain the children had made their own clay models, put them on the family shrine, and offered gifts of rice to them, decorating them with garlands; after a day or two they were dissolved in water. But there was no procession, and they rather missed that part of it.

Sumitra remembered some of the stories of Ganesha, which Ma used to tell her. She was especially fond of the story of the way Ganesha came to have an elephant's head. It all went back to a time when Shiva, the great god, returned from a long period of meditation in the forest. Parvati, his wife, had set their son to guard the door while she had a bath. Now Shiva had left before his son was born, so when he was challenged by the boy on his return, he did not recognize him and unfortunately struck off his

12. Ganesha, the elephant-headed god. The cobra and the trident are symbols of the great god Shiva, the father of Ganesha. The axe is a symbol of power; one hand is raised in blessing.

head in anger. When he realized what he had done and the head could not be found, he ordered a servant to go into the forest and bring back the head of whoever met him first. As it happened it was an elephant who had loved the little boy and was only too glad to sacrifice his head to bring the boy back to life. Although Shiva was at first ashamed of his son with an elephant's head, he gave him the name of Ganesha, chief of the lesser gods.

Krishna remembered the statue of Ganesha which they had in their house in Gujarat when he was quite a small boy, and how his mother had explained to him that a statue of Ganesha in an Indian house still serves to remind people that God is not only patient, strong and wise, like the elephant, but also is to be found as much in things we find ugly as those we find beautiful.

The stories of Krishna and Ganesha were somewhat puzzling to Peter and Susan. Why so many gods? Why so many statues? Mr. Patel tried to explain that Hindus believe that God, known as Brahman, really lives everywhere as Spirit. He doesn't have a shape you can see and touch but, so that human beings may have a better chance of understanding him, he appears on earth in many different forms, human or animal, male or female. Peter and Susan still found it hard to understand, but thought it might become clearer as they got to know their Hindu friends better.

Mr Patel then told them that the special symbol Hindus have for God is the sound *Om* which, when it is written in the sacred language of Sanskrit, looks like this:

13. *Om*, the sacred symbol of God.

MORNING PUJA IN THE PATEL HOUSEHOLD

Although Hindus like to go as often as they can to the temple to join in worship with other people, it is really the home which is the centre of their religion. Here the members of the family may perform their own devotions in whatever way they choose. The Hindu word for worship is *Puja*. If they have a house large enough, a room may be set aside for Puja, a place for quietness and meditation. The Patels did not have any room to spare, so they simply hung pictures of Krishna in the living-room, while upstairs each member of the family had a shelf or a table on which stood a statue or a picture of their chosen god.

Like most Indian families, the Patels rise early in the morning. Mr. Patel first shaves, then has a thorough wash, no quick wipe of the face and hands. When he has saved enough money he will install a shower unit; meanwhile he simply pours water over himself in the bath. It is important to wash carefully because the body must be clean and the worshipper in the right frame of mind before he says his prayers. The women in the family — Ma, Mrs. Patel and Kamala — put on clean saris after washing, and brush and oil their hair, twisting it into a knot with a flower to decorate it. They touch their foreheads with sandalwood and vermilion paste to mark a small red spot between their eyes; this is called a *tilak* or *kumkum* mark. Often it is simply used as make-up, but it has also a deeper meaning. It is often called the third eye of wisdom and spiritual sight, and is to remind them of the presence of God as they come to worship, and as they go about their daily work.

On Mr. Patel's table is a statue of Krishna and Radha, and on either side pictures of Ganesha and a Gujarati saint called Jalaram. There are also two holy books: the Bhagavata Purana which tells the story of Krishna's life, and the Gita. As he comes to his Puja, he first rings the small bell which stands on the table, and then he washes the statue with *panchamrit* (a mixture of milk, yoghurt, sugar, honey, and *ghee* which is clarified or melted butter), cleaning it afterwards with water and drying it. Then he puts on the statue and the pictures a little *haldi* (turmeric powder, also used in cooking), and *kumkum* and also a little rice.

He lays some flowers and rice in front of the statue, and smears a tiny bit of sandalwood paste on it as well. He offers these things to show his gratitude to God who provides all things. He then traces with his finger a *mandala* (a square shape) and places his prasad (his gift to God) in the mandala.

Now he stands still, concentrating on controlling his breathing; this helps him to relax and think more clearly. The incense sticks are lit, providing a sweet scent and reminding him of his prayers as they rise to God.

Finally the Arti lamp is lit. It consists of a small earthenware bowl in which he places some cotton wool soaked in *ghee* and neatly twisted into a wick.

One of the gods is Agni, the god of fire, and this lighted lamp is to show that God is present. Now he says his prayers, especially to Ganesha and

14. A household shrine.

Krishna. To help him concentrate he repeats some of the names of God, saying *Hare Krishna, Hare Krishna, Krishna Krishna, Hare Hare.* (*Hare* is another name of the God Vishnu.) Finally he remembers that God is everywhere by turning in every direction, joining his hands and asking God's blessing on the day to come.

His prayers have taken him about twenty minutes and he is now ready for his breakfast and the day's work. Of course many Hindus, who are not so religious or have not enough time, may simply pause beside a picture or statue of a god, light an incense stick, say one or two prayers and set off for work. There are no set rules about praying, and if you have very little time to set aside it doesn't matter; God will understand. All that a Hindu is required to do each day is to worship God by thinking quietly about him, and by performing the Puja ritual before one of the images of God, like Krishna or Ganesha; to show respect for old people and those who have died; to offer hospitality to all guests and give to those in need; and to care for and feed animals and birds. (These are known as the 'five daily duties'.)

A NEW ARRIVAL

Much to the delight of the family Mrs. Patel was expecting a baby. In Gujarat there would have been many ceremonies; at the start of the fifth month of pregnancy the husband would offer *panchamrit* to his wife, the offering presented to a god in worship or to an honoured guest; after all, the baby was a gift from God and should be treated as an honoured guest.

Not long after the time when all the unborn child's limbs were fully formed, though still very small, there would be the ceremony of the parting of the wife's hair. This was done to prepare her for the birth and make her safe from the attack of evil spirits which might try to harm her child.

It is necessary to have a priest to conduct all such ceremonies. (They are known as *samskaras*.) As it is often not possible to get a Brahmin priest to come, Hindus in Britain generally only keep four of these ceremonies: the naming ceremony, the first haircut, marriage and the funeral rites.

The baby was born at the hospital while Mr. Patel was away on business; but the news was telephoned through to him that he was the father of another son, and he came to visit as soon as he was able. As the hospital sister was from India and understood their customs, he was allowed to do what should have been done at the time of birth, and touched the lips of the child with a spoonful of honey and ghee, praying for blessing on the new life.

They had already agreed to have the naming ceremony performed, so a Brahmin priest who lived in a nearby town was informed of the date and time of birth. This is important because Hindus believe that the life of every person is controlled by the exact positions of the planets and constellations at the moment of birth.

The priest prepares the child's *janmapatrika* (the horoscope), recording the time of birth, the positions of the planets and constellations, and the parents' names. He may also refer to the family tree. He had suggested three or four suitable names, and they had agreed what it should be before the ceremony.

Preparations were made for the event on a Sunday ten days after the birth, shortly after Mrs. Patel and the baby came home. A number of relatives and friends, including the Clarkes, were invited. Ma had of course taken charge of the household whilst Mrs. Patel was in hospital, and now she was busy making arrangements for the weekend.

The short naming ceremony was held in the living room of their home, a happy family occasion. The priest announced that his name was to be Deepak, which means 'Light'. This name, according to an ancient tradition, should begin with a letter from the word referring to the star under which he had been born. They had had to choose a name beginning with either a 'd' or a 'ch', so the name Deepak was acceptable. In India the baby would then have been taken outside the house to be shown the sunlight for the first time, but the weather was too cold and damp, so the ceremony ended with some prayers from the Vedas, and then Mr. Patel distributed presents all round to the family and the guests. They then sat down to a meal together before going home.

Seeing that Mr. Clarke was becoming very interested Mr. Patel was very pleased to explain as much as he could. The next ceremony (kept by most people in India) was the cutting of the first lock of hair.

THE FIRST HAIRCUT

Between the ages of two and five, when most children are learning to talk properly, exploring new things and causing all sorts of trouble for their mothers, there is a special ceremony to mark this occasion. This is only for boys; most girls and women never cut their hair. Hindus believe that shaving and hair-cutting are signs of cleansing of body and soul. In days gone by all the priests used to shave the head completely except for one tuft. You will still see holy men in India with heads shaved like that. You may well have seen the shaven heads of young men of the Hare Krishna movement in the cities of Britain, dressed in yellow robes and chanting 'Hare Krishna' as they walk the pavements.

The haircut marks the first important stage of learning and growing up. Krishna had this special haircut when the family were living in Gujarat, but the Patels had decided that Deepak should not go through this ceremony. Some families, like the Sharmas who were friends of the Patels, took their young son all the way back to their home in Gujarat for the ceremony, which of course cost them a great deal of money. Mr. Sharma's mother still lived in Gujarat, and it was her wish that they should go; so, despite the cost, how could Mr. Sharma deny his mother the chance to see her son and her grandson?

34

THE SACRED THREAD CEREMONY

Many years ago the *Yagyopavit* or 'sacred thread ceremony' was very important for all Hindus, except the lowest caste. Nowadays, although some Hindus keep up the tradition in India, it is often only the Brahmins (the highest caste) who do so in Britain. It happened that a Brahmin was visiting the Patels, and he agreed to tell the Clarkes about it; he had conducted the ceremony for a family in the Midlands earlier that year. He told them of his own initiation; for that was what he called it. ('Initiation' means a beginning and an introduction to something new.)

'From my earliest years', he said, 'I learnt about the gods, and my grandma told me the stories of Rama and Sita, and of Krishna, and I learnt to pray at the shrine in our home. They used to take me to the temple as often as they could. It is said that a Hindu learns to pray and meditate first through respect for his mother, then for his father, and finally for his *guru* (his religious teacher). When I reached the age of eight, my father said that I was ready to receive the sacred thread and start my religious education with a special teacher. This was a big moment for me, as for every Hindu boy, because up to then I had been considered only a child, and spent most of my time with my mother, grandma and the other women of the family. Now I was to be recognized as one of the adults, and would have to learn to behave like an adult, and start to understand the holy writings of the Hindus. This initiation ceremony is often called a second birth; your first birth is physical, your second birth is spiritual, because you are no longer a child and are beginning to understand more about the world and your place in it. It is usually only the boys who are initiated, although there is sometimes a similar ceremony for girls.

'My parents invited relatives and friends to attend the ceremony with the family. I washed very carefully, had my hair trimmed and my nails cut; then dressed in a white *dhoti* (which consists of one piece of white cloth wound between the legs and around the waist) I sat with my parents beside the family shrine. The priest offered fruit and sweetmeats to the god, and lit the Sacred Fire. On important occasions, happy or sad, offerings are made to the Sacred Fire whose flames represent the life, purity and power of God. I was seated on one side of the fire with my father, and the priest on the other side. He began to chant prayers, asking Agni the god of fire to

35

witness the ceremony. Guided by the priest, I offered ghee and sesame seeds to the fire, and prayed to the gods to make me pure and worthy of the spiritual initiation.

'The priest then whispered in my ear a *mantra* (a holy word with special meaning) which I was to remember and think about when I performed my daily worship, and, taking the sacred thread, he hung it over my left shoulder, passing the ends round my body next to the skin and tying them under my right arm. This thread is made of three strands intertwined to remind the Hindu of God who shows himself in the world in three forms, that is as Brahma, Vishnu and Shiva.

'He then said the Gayatri Mantra and I was required to repeat the words after him.

These are the words:

> Let us meditate on the most excellent light of the Creator. May he guide our minds, and inspire us with understanding.

This prayer is as important to Hindus as the Lord's Prayer is to Christians, and is heard at most religious ceremonies. I promised to undertake the duties of a man, and to live a life devoted to God. I sat in meditation for a while repeating the mantra which he had given to me. After this I had to go to my relatives to beg for the day's meal. This was done because in India in days gone by the young boy then set off for some time on his own, wandering from village to village or living in the open air with his guru and learning from him. All this time they would live by begging food from villagers, as many holy men do to this day in India.

'Finally, I asked a blessing from the priest, my parents and relatives. Then a dinner was served to all the guests.

'After the ceremony I was required to repeat the mantra and meditate before breakfast and the evening meal every day. During the next few years I was to learn from my guru how to conduct all the household and temple ceremonies and what they meant.

'So you see, I was now a much more important person in the family, and my father and his friends began to treat me as a grown-up. The next time I went to the temple, I walked with the men of the family while the women and the girls followed behind.'

Mr. Patel said that his family, who were from the Vaishya caste, did not practise this ceremony, but he added that there were some Vaishyas who did so in London and in the Midlands, and maybe more families would in the future.

THE FESTIVAL OF *NAVA RATRI* OR *DURGA PUJA*

Every autumn there were celebrations in honour of Durga, the Divine Mother. Preparations were made well ahead, and since even the Hindu Centre was not big enough for the crowds a larger school hall was booked for the week. Krishna and Sumitra were going every evening with their parents, and it was soon arranged that Peter and Susan should go with them one evening, and their parents too if they could.

Sumitra told them that during the week the family showed extra special respect for their mother, and remembered with gratitude that it was she who had given birth to them, and spent almost all her time looking after them, cooking their food, mending their clothes, and comforting them when they were hurt or upset. Hindus are expected to show as much respect for their mothers as they do for God. Susan was reminded of Mothering Sunday in the spring, when they made a special posy of flowers or a greetings card for their mother, and Peter took her a cup of tea in bed. Her mother told her that it used to be the custom for Christians to revisit their 'mother church', the one in which they were brought up as children, and to return to their family home, bringing presents for their mothers; by tradition this present was a bunch of violets and a 'simnel' cake (a rich fruit cake rather like a Christmas cake).

Sumitra decided to call their *Nava Ratri* (which means 'nine nights') by the new name of 'Mothering Week', as the two festivals seemed to be celebrating much the same thing.

The Clarkes were not free to go till the Friday evening, and they went down to the hall together with the Patels. All the Indians in the town were going, or so it seemed, so they simply followed the crowd. There was an air of excitement; the hall was very quickly filling up with families, all dressed in their very best clothes for the occasion. It was a happy reunion for many families, because their married daughters had come home to spend a while with their parents. Kamala (Sumitra's sister) was already chatting away to her friends who had married in the spring, and were now staying at home for a while.

Every year they would return like this in the autumn, if they were able; for some this was the first visit home since the wedding, so their families

37

and friends were making a great fuss of them. Kamala's best friend, Sita, was proudly showing off her sari, which her mother had given her as a 'coming home' present. It had cost a great deal of money, but it showed how pleased they were to welcome her home again.

In the centre of the hall a six-sided shrine had been set up. On each of the sides was a picture of a goddess, each a different way of seeing God as Mother. One was Lakshmi, the goddess of prosperity; another was Saraswati, the goddess of learning and intelligence, and so on. As they worshipped, they would remember that success in education and in work comes from God, and it is God to whom we should pray for help in these matters.

Some of the older women, including Ma, were beginning to light the incense-sticks and the small ghee lamps, and set them in front of the pictures of the goddesses. A group of musicians started to beat out a strong rhythm on the *tabla* (a small drum) and the singers soon joined in with traditional Gujarati songs. A few children started to circle the shrine, led by a young man who was showing them the steps, singing the songs and clapping his hands as he danced to the rhythmic beat of the drum. Soon more joined the line, and before long there were three circles of dancers of all ages, clapping and swaying as they danced anti-clockwise around the shrine. The men and boys danced in the inner ring, and in the outer rings were the women and the girls. They all joined in together, the grandmothers moved round sedately, the teenagers moved to the music with great enthusiasm, enjoying every minute of it, the younger women obviously showing off their brightly coloured saris, while the young children (some only three or four years old) followed the steps hesitantly, but with obvious pride in the fact that they were joining in with the grown-ups. The Clarkes were at once invited to join in the dance too, and tried to follow the steps and the clapping — without much success; but that did not matter, and it was all good fun.

By this time the hall was packed to capacity; it was just like a discotheque — the sound of the singing and the drums made it almost impossible to carry on any sort of conversation. The louder the music, the more enthusiastic was the dancing; the tabla player would change the tempo, and the dancers, all in unison, would catch the mood, and increase the speed of the steps as they whirled around the floor.

All this was enjoyable and very exhausting, but it was much more than that to many of them. The songs, the steps of the dance and the rhythm of the drums were all ways of showing respect and devotion to the Divine Mother, God, who provides us with everything we need.

38

For a while there was a lull in the proceedings, as the winners of the evening's raffle were announced, but almost as soon as this was completed two circles of women and children gathered round the shrine and prepared for the evening *arti*. Groups of women and children carried trays on which were placed several ghee lamps, and they circled the shrine, the lamps flickering as they moved round, and the incense sticks sending spirals of smoke into the air. The entire audience sang the hymns to the Divine Mother, clapping in perfect unison. A quarter of an hour had passed, and still the singing and chanting continued; the drum beat became fast and furious, the worshippers still circled the shrine. One old lady was so carried away by her devotion, as she swayed to the music, that eventually she sank to the floor exhausted, and others, recognizing how devoted she was to God, bowed down before her in respect.

The prayers were over, and in no time at all the dancers appeared again, this time holding short sticks (called *dandiyas*) which were decorated with coloured tassels ready for the stick dancing. They were now dancing in pairs, the men with men, the women with women, striking their partners' sticks as they changed places. The hall resounded to the crash of the sticks and the beat of the drums; there were plenty of broken sticks before the dances were finished! The evening ended in great excitement as most of the audience took part, and there was hardly room for the dancers to move without bumping into someone.

It was time to leave, but not before everyone had been given their prasad, a small bag of nuts, raisins, sugar crystals, apple, coconut and sweets. Groups of families drifted home down the dimly lit streets, tired but happy and eager to return the next evening for the last and most important day of the festival. This was called *Dussehra*, when they were to remember the time when Rama destroyed the demon king Ravana and the forces of evil, and brought Sita home to Ayodhya in triumph.

ONE LIFE ENDS AND ANOTHER BEGINS

Dadaji and Ma had come to Britain soon after the Patels had settled, as Dadaji wanted to be with his son and daughter-in-law as he grew older. He and his wife had spent the best part of their lives bringing up their family, and they had sacrificed many pleasures. Now it was their son's duty to look after them. There is rarely any need to send anyone to an old people's home, for in a Hindu family someone will always be found to take care of them in their old age. He had enjoyed a long and happy life, and was now seventy-two years old. It had given him great pleasure a few days before to stand and watch his family celebrating the Durga Puja.

But now he was not so well; he had caught a bad cold in the damp weather, the cold had turned into bronchitis, and a few days later he died. His last days had been happy because he had his family beside him; whenever they were free they sat with him to keep him company. Mrs. Patel sometimes found time to read to him from the Gita; Dadaji was too tired to do anything but listen and watch his family as they went about their work in the house. It was a sad time, in one way, but Dadaji was quite content to leave this life, because like all Hindus he believed that his spirit would not die. In fact, his spirit had lived in some other body before he was born seventy-two years ago, and when he died would pass to another body. This is usually called 're-incarnation'. Hindus believe that bad deeds in one life receive their punishment in the next, while good deeds give you a good start in the next life.

Dadaji had lived a good life and been blessed with a happy family, and knew that his *karma* (his actions) would result in his spirit's passing to a healthy body in the next life. He was much comforted, as were all his family, by these words from the Gita:

> As a man leaves his old clothes and puts on new ones, so the spirit leaves his body and moves to a new one. . . His spirit doesn't die when the body dies, for all things born, in truth, must die; and out of death, in truth, comes life. Face to face with what must be, cease from sorrow.

As his last moments came, they tried to turn his thoughts to God by chanting the words *Ram bolo bha Ram*, that is, 'Say, brother, Ram, Ram'. Hindus believe that dying with a name of God on your lips will bring you closer to God. His lips were touched with water containing the leaves of the sacred *Tulsi* plant.

At the point of death, naturally, the family wept; but to show too much emotion is thought to disturb his spirit, so they quickly set about making the arrangements for the funeral. The family read from the scriptures and sang hymns beside his body, but because death causes 'uncleanness' in the house, the daily worship was suspended for a while.

Hindus always cremate their dead, so in India the body would have been taken, within a day, to the 'burning ghat' (which is really just an open-air crematorium) and a coffin would not have been necessary. But in Britain things are done differently: the body was washed, wrapped in cloth, and placed in a coffin at the undertaker's. As they believed that his spirit was still attached to human things, although it had left the body, the members of the family showed their respect and love for Dadaji by putting in the coffin some rice, a coin or two, ghee, coconut, jasmine and red tilak powder. Then they covered the body with a new piece of red cloth. (Red is the colour of life, and is used both at weddings and at funerals. After all, death is the beginning of a new life, not the end of everything.)

When the funeral party arrived at the crematorium, the male relatives helped to carry the coffin into the chapel. There was a short ceremony. They had arranged for an Indian priest to officiate, and he read from the scriptures and said the funeral prayers. He read from the second chapter of the Gita, and repeated slowly the words which they had read to Dadaji shortly before he had died:

> As a man leaves his old clothes, and puts on new ones, so the spirit leaves his body and moves to a new one . . .

As they believed that the body returns again into the five elements, as it were 'dust to dust, and ashes to ashes', he prayed these words just before the body was cremated:

> May your eyesight return to the sun, your breath to the winds, may your waters mingle with the ocean and your earthly parts become one with the earth.

In India it was the duty — a very important one — of the eldest son in the family to light the funeral pyre: at the crematorium Mr. Patel was allowed to stand by the coffin, and put his hand on it as it moved through the doors towards the furnace.

The priest ended the ceremony with a blessing, used on many occasions, saying the words:

> Brahman, the Supreme, is Peace.
> May all be in Peace, in Peace and only in Peace,
> and may that Peace come unto me.
> Om, Peace, Peace, Peace.

On the third day some of the ashes were collected from the crematorium, put in a special container, and sent back to India, there to be scattered in the holy river Ganga (Ganges) by another member of the family.

During the first ten days after the funeral, according to the custom, the family were able only to eat simple food; the Patels made special offerings of rice at their home shrine, and in the house they wore only white clothing.

All this was to show the spirit of Dadaji that the family was grateful for kind acts done in his life, and to help the spirit on to its next birth.

There was a custom that on the eleventh day the eldest son should shave his head, but Mr. Patel had a light haircut instead. The thirteenth day marked the end of mourning, and many friends were invited to a meal. After that life returned to normal, and they simply made offerings of rice once a month to remember the dead.

DIWALI, THE NEW YEAR FESTIVAL OF LIGHTS

Once more it was November, and time for the Festival of Diwali, when Hindus come together to celebrate the arrival of the New Year with entertainments and festivities. It is sometimes called *Deepawali*; (*deepa* or *deepak* means a 'light' or 'lamp'). In Britain as in India people of other religions, too, like Sikhs and Christians, gladly accept invitations to join in these celebrations.

It wasn't very long since the festival of Dussehra, when they had remembered the victory of Rama over the evil forces of Ravana. Now the Patels, like all the Hindus in the town, were preparing to celebrate the time when Rama and Sita returned to their kingdom in triumph and, after a long period of trouble and unhappiness and poverty, the goddess Lakshmi came down to them to bring peace and prosperity again.

Mr. Patel and his family always said prayers together that day, and one of the prayers they said was this one:

From the unreal lead me to the real,
From darkness lead me to the light,
From death lead me to immortality .

When Lakshmi comes, it is said, she will not visit the homes unless they are lighted with lamps, and cleaned ready for her coming. So everywhere the lamps were shining brightly in the Patel's house. A lamp had been hung outside the front door, and the front window was decorated with coloured light bulbs, just as at Christmas time. Sumitra and her mother had been busy during the day giving the house a special Diwali clean. She carried Deepak, still of course a small baby, round the house to show him the

42

15. A dancer with sparklers at the festival of Diwali.

lamps. As his name meant 'light', this festival would have a special meaning for him when he was old enough to understand things for himself.

By the time it was dusk there were lights throughout the house, not only light bulbs but also rows of little ghee lamps, lighting up all the dark corners of the rooms. Lakshmi would hardly be likely to miss out their house!

During the summer Mr. Patel had changed his job, and was now running a grocery business at a small corner shop; so there was no shortage of lamps and ghee, as they sold a lot of these things in their shop. The previous February, during an electricity strike, all their lighting had come from these small cotton-wick lamps, which had made it seem like Diwali.

But now it really was Diwali, and for the first time in his new business, as the custom was, he settled all the old accounts and started new ones for the New Year.

Diwali is always a time to exchange gifts, and the children could hardly wait until they were given their presents. Every one had some new clothes for the occasion; Krishna had a brightly coloured shirt and trousers to match, and of course Sumitra was given a length of material for a sari. Mrs. Patel would never let Diwali go by, if she could help it, without buying herself a sari. She had a very large selection of them by now.

On the mantelpiece in their living room there were a few Diwali cards, for it was customary to send greetings cards to people, just as British families do at Christmas time, and to give money to charities.

The Gujarati Hindu Society had that year arranged to hold their New Year celebrations in a big way. There was to be an evening's entertainment in the large concert hall of the new Guildhall which seated several thousand people. Mr. Patel was responsible for organizing the entertainment, and he had hardly a moment to himself in the week before it.

On the evening the hall was filled to capacity, with people coming from a number of the surrounding towns as well as their own, and many guests from the town — a town councillor, a manager of a factory where many Gujaratis worked, and some teachers who had come to see their pupils perform traditional dances. The Clarkes were all there. Peter and Susan went round backstage with Krishna and Sumitra to see them prepare for their part in the programme, while Mr. and Mrs. Clarke sat with Mrs. Patel and Ma.

The programme began with a parade of children who came in in pairs, one boy with one girl, each pair dressed in the traditional costume of a part of India. Krishna and Sumitra were in Gujarati costume and, of course,

16. Dancing at the Diwali celebrations.

were greeted with a specially loud cheer as they joined the colourful display of Indian dress as it was spotlighted on the stage. As they all stood there two more children, dressed as the Lord Krishna and Radha his companion, went forward to light the Diwali lamp and welcome the New Year on behalf of the whole audience.

For several hours there was a succession of singing, dancing and speeches, and the hall buzzed with the sound of excited youngsters as they ran around with their friends, making the most of the carnival atmosphere and finding time to eat and drink as often as they could persuade their parents to part with some more money. Diwali was obviously an occasion on which to eat and drink and have a thoroughly enjoyable time, but it would be a pity to forget the real meaning of the festival.

It is around the *deepak* (lamp) that the festival revolves. The lamp symbolizes the banishment of the darkness of evil and ignorance. The bright flame is the symbol of a pure heart, which has been enlightened by the knowledge of God. The cleaning of the home represents the purity of their hearts, and the wearing of new clothes represents the new life that comes to their hearts. The settling of old accounts and the starting of new ones reminds them all that from this day of Diwali all quarrels and bad habits should be put behind them, and a new leaf turned over.

When you light the Diwali lamps, you should remember that it is really the lamp of your heart that has to be lit, so that the goddess Lakshmi may come to stay in your heart. A good Hindu, whose heart is pure and whose body and mind are clean, is like the flame of the Diwali lamp burning clearly and steadily.

THE SUNDAY FILMS

Every Sunday, from noon until early evening, Indian films were shown at one of the cinemas in the town. The Patels did not go very often, but when they did it was a good chance to see a film about their own country and hear their own language. Ma in particular liked the films because as she watched them she was carried back to her childhood. At least for two hours she was far away in her village, gossiping to her neighbours and watching the world go by, drinking in the warmth of the sun and listening to those familiar sounds, the sharp chattering of the monkeys as they jumped from roof to roof and the soft lowing of the cows as they plodded quietly along the street.

But all too soon the film was over, the spell was broken, and she was back once more in Britain and walking home with Sumitra.

HOLI — THE FESTIVAL OF SPRING

The long months of wet, cold weather had often made Ma homesick for the warmth of the Indian sun. As February and March came and went and the blustery winds and flurries of snow gave way to warmer spring days, she began to talk about the festival of *Holi* which her people in Gujarat would soon be celebrating.

All that Krishna could remember was the lighting of the bonfire and getting covered with mud and coloured water. Both Peter and Susan, when they heard about it, secretly hoped that Holi would be celebrated at the Hindu Centre, and that they would be able to go. As it happened, Mr. Patel told them that they were not able to build a bonfire as there was not enough room for it behind the buildings; he hoped they would be able to find a suitable place for it another year. This was a disappointment of course, but Sumitra later told Susan that Ma was so keen on Holi that,

17. Indian films.

when she found out that the festival was to be held in a nearby town, she had persuaded Mr. Patel to take them all there to join in the festivities. It had not been difficult to persuade him, for it would have been unthinkable for him to refuse a request like that from his own mother.

Quite a large party set off on the Sunday afternoon. Mrs. Patel had advised the Clarkes to wear old clothes. Krishna and Sumitra were as excited as Peter and Susan, for it was two years since they had been to a Holi bonfire.

On the way Mrs. Patel told them the story of Prahlada and the demoness Holika. 'Once, long ago, even the gods were afraid of some evil demons who had gained control of the world. They begged the great god Vishnu to help them, and he did so in a very strange way.

'The king of the demons, called Hiranyakashipu, had declared that all demons and men must worship him alone. Soon after, a son was born to him. He was named Prahlada. To his father's disgust Prahlada turned out to be a very religious boy. So a teacher was employed to make sure that all ideas of God were put out of his mind. But when he was taught the alphabet, he would say that *K* stood for Krishna, *V* stood for Vishnu and *G* stood for Gopala (a nickname for Krishna). Nothing would move him

47

from his worship of Krishna, and he steadfastly refused to promise to give up his worship. The king tried all sorts of punishments and tortures to persuade him, but all of them failed. Finally he asked his sister Holika to come to his aid. Now Holika had been given magical power which enabled her to pass through fire unharmed. So she took Prahlada in her arms and entered the fire. But to the king's dismay, Holika was burnt to ashes, because her power remained only if she entered the fire alone, while Prahlada was unhurt because he continued chanting *Hare Krishna* all the time he was in the fire.'

When the party arrived at the Shri Krishna temple, they left their shoes at the door and entered the temple to join the crowds already gathering inside. It was very like their own Prayer Hall, with the main shrine dedicated to Lord Krishna. The crowd inside were chanting the names of the Lord Krishna. Mr. Patel explained that they were all following the example of the young boy Prahlada who had shown his great devotion in the same way.

Incense filled the temple and the priest rang the bell as he prepared for Arti. He offered food, fire, water and incense to Krishna. As he did so, the chanting echoed through the temple, 'Praise to the Supreme Lord for saving your worshippers from the trials and troubles of this world'.

By now the children were becoming restless, anxious to get out to the bonfire. They didn't have to wait long, for the grown-ups were almost as keen to get out. The fire was just being set alight; to Peter and Susan it was just like Guy Fawkes day all over again. A large effigy of Holika with a hideous face had been securely fixed on a frame at the top of the pile. The fire was burning fiercely, and the flames were licking the figure of Holika. In a short while the figure began to totter, and a loud cheer greeted the fall of the wicked demoness as she collapsed in the flames and was reduced to ashes. Once more evil had been conquered.

The fire was now red-hot and a number of coconuts were placed in the ashes to roast, as the people chanted prayers to Agni the god of fire. When the coconuts were ready they were carefully picked out by the men, and the boys rushed forward eagerly to help to crack them so that the delicious pieces could be shared out. (It is an old tradition that only the men and boys are allowed to do this.)

Coconuts are a symbol of good luck. They are a complete natural food, providing milk, carbohydrate and protein — all that we need. When offering a coconut to God, it is as if we are saying, 'We are giving the most valuable thing we have, to show our love for God'.

48

18. Women carry their young children round the bonfire at the festival of Holi.

Mrs. Clarke noticed a young mother carrying her baby round the fire; she did so five times. She asked Mrs. Patel why, and she told her that the young woman would be praying to Agni to give her son success in his life. The fire was dying down and the people were beginning to move away. This was the moment Krishna, along with many others, had been waiting for. All of a sudden they found themselves being squirted with coloured water, amid shrieks of laughter and screams of mock surprise. Sumitra gave Susan a bucket of water and a bicycle pump, and told her to squirt it at anyone who came within range. She didn't need a second invitation and was soon spraying coloured water in all directions with gay abandon. Ma was to be seen smearing charcoal on another lady's face and being daubed with mud in return, clearly enjoying every minute of it; for a few moments she was reliving the carefree days of her childhood.

Back into the hall they went to dry themselves, while some remained by the fire for a while. Then they sat down to a meal of rice and chapattis, and a cup of hot sweet tea which was most welcome after the excitement of the evening.

As the Clarkes and Patels had some way to go, they left earlier than most and travelled back home. Of course Sumitra had to explain to them why they always squirted water at each other: she said that they were

49

celebrating the return of the Lord Krishna to his home in Brindaban, where he used to play his flute and sing and dance with the milkmaids. They were remembering the time when the cowherds covered the milkmaids with milk and turmeric powder, and the milkmaids retaliated with red Kumkum powder.

Nowadays it is a day for childish pranks and practical jokes; it is a custom that up to midday everyone is equal, and children tease parents, employees play jokes on their employers and pupils may make fun of their teachers. Peter was not slow to wonder whether they could introduce that practice at school! The nearest they ever got to it was April Fools' Day.

They arrived home late, weary but happy after a never-to-be-forgotten experience. It was the first time that Peter and Susan had enjoyed two bonfire nights in one winter.

KAMALA'S WEDDING

Back at school Sumitra was excitedly telling Susan of her elder sister's wedding which was to take place the Sunday after next at the Hindu Centre. Imagine her delight when, a few days later, Sumitra brought an invitation to the wedding. The card was colourfully decorated; on it was the figure of Ganesha. As he removed obstacles and brought good fortune, no one would think of arranging a wedding without first praying to him for success.

Preparations for the wedding had been under way for some months. As soon as Mr. and Mrs. Patel had realized that Kamala wished to marry Govinda, they had sent a family friend to find out whether he was suitable for her. When Sumitra's mother had been married, everything had been arranged by her parents, and she didn't actually see her future husband until the wedding. Kamala's parents knew that Govinda belonged to the same caste, but they still had to consult their family pandit who knew the history of their family and would know whether his life horoscope matched hers. They sent for photographs of Govinda and made enquiries about his health, his education, his job and how much he earned.

Hindus believe that marriage is far too important to be left to the chance of falling in love. Young people may fall in love without thinking, maybe after only meeting two or three times. If they marry quickly, it is quite likely that they will find out that they were not really suited after all and will wish to live apart. Parents know their children better than anyone else, and

19. A Hindu wedding scene.

are concerned for their happiness, so they help in choosing a suitable partner. If possible, all the family, grandparents, and other relatives and friends should agree on the choice.

When they were quite sure that it was right to arrange a marriage between the two families, they sent a gift of money to Govinda's parents and started to make preparations. Many ceremonies followed: in the presence of a priest and friends and relations the fathers of the couple signed a document, which included a family tree of both families for three generations back. Then the men of the bride's family met with the pandit to decide on the most favourable day for the wedding. It was decided to hold it on the last day of April.

By the time Sumitra arrived at the Centre on the day of the wedding, she was already quite tired because, since early that morning, their house had been the scene of feverish activity as the women of the household prepared the bride for her wedding. Kamala was given a special bath; prayers were said; then she was dressed in a beautiful red sari with real gold thread running through it. (Most brides wear red, the colour of life.) She then put on all her ornaments, necklaces, bangles and anklets. Finally the *tilak* was applied to her forehead, and grains of rice were stuck to the red paste as a sign of blessing. Susan wanted to see her straight away, but

Sumitra said that she had to sit alone with her mother in a side-room until the bridegroom arrived.

The hall was already crowded when they entered. In the centre was a large canopy supported by four poles and decorated with coloured paper and balloons; on the side in Sanskrit was painted the sign *Om* (see page 30). The women and children were sitting on one side of the canopy, and the men on the other side; there was a buzz of conversation. At last there was a stir, and heads were turned to the door. Three coaches had arrived from London, bringing the bridegroom and his party. A girl from the bride's family, with a coconut held gracefully on her head by a scarf, walked slowly to the door to meet the bridegroom who had now been joined by the bride. Sumitra and Susan found some chairs to stand on, and had a grandstand view as the priest chanted mantras and threw rice over the couple, and the women sang a song of welcome.

Coming to the canopy, where two special seats were set for them, the bride was led to her place by an uncle. Together they stood in front of the priest, the bride on the left of the bridegroom, while an offering was made to Ganesha at the small shrine to make sure that all went well. The priest warned them that marriage was not to be undertaken lightly; they would be required to share all they had, and to sacrifice many things for their family. If they wanted to change their minds, he said, now was the time to do it.

The bride's father then gave away his daughter to the bridegroom, and the ritual began. Every wedding must be witnessed by Agni, the god of fire, who is the symbol of the sun and power. So a fire, the Sacred Fire, was lit in a metal container. The priest put ghee on the sticks before setting light to it. Throughout the ritual the priest and the couple continued to add ghee, as well as rice and coconut kernel to the fire to keep it going. The priest then took a sheet of white linen and fastened one end of it to the bridegroom's clothes, and the other end to the bride's clothes. After the linen had been removed and they had been garlanded with flowers, he joined their hands together, chanting prayers as he did so, while the bride's elder brother poured rice over their hands. Next he took a cord and placed it around their shoulders. These actions were to show that marriage was a union of two souls which should not be broken. There were many scriptures to be read, much water to be sprinkled and red powder thrown. At last the priest told them to stand and the bridegroom, linked to the bride by the cord, led her round the fire several times. The guests watched all that happened very carefully, but at no time did they have to sit still and silent; in fact Sumitra and Susan moved more than once to

20. Rice is thrown on the couple's hands at their wedding.

get a better view, and in the middle of one long prayer there was a loud bang when a young man burst a balloon which was hanging from the canopy. Then suddenly a woman began a cheerful song, and the women around her joined in the chorus. Susan wanted to know what it was all about; Sumitra told her that it was a wedding song, telling of the beauty of the bride and the handsome bridegroom. Catching sight of some drinks, she darted along a row of chairs and came back with two beakers of coca-cola.

But now came the most important part of the ceremony. At a nod from the priest, the bride, followed by the bridegroom, took the 'Seven Steps' (*Saptapadi*) around the Sacred Fire, keeping the fire on their right and making promises at each step to honour and respect each other. As he went Govinda said,

> Take one step for food, two for strength, three for increasing wealth, four for good fortune, five for children, six for the seasons and in seven steps be my friend . . .

The words which Sumitra liked best were spoken by the bridegroom to the bride earlier in the ceremony. They were chanted in Sanskrit, but her father had told her what they meant:

> I take hold of your hand for good fortune, so that with me as your husband you may live to old age. I am the words, you are the melody; I am the melody, you are the words.

Govinda had promised not to ask for any gifts in addition to the dowry which Kamala's parents had given. He had promised to provide Kamala with a good home, food, clothing and all she needed; to consult her before spending a lot of money, and to take her with him when he went out in his leisure time, whenever he could.

Kamala in her turn had promised to obey him and be faithful to him. She had undertaken not to take back money and belongings to her parents' home, but to devote herself fully to looking after her new home and family.

Govinda and Kamala were now husband and wife. The priest addressed the couple, telling them of their duties. He made several jokes about husbands and wives, and mothers-in-law, which caused much amusement among the guests. When this was over, relatives and friends queued up to congratulate the couple and bring their gifts, often dabbing more red paste on their tilaks and sticking grains of rice on them. The family sat by to receive the gifts, and Sumitra helped to pile the parcels neatly in a corner when a note had been made of their contents and the name of the donor.

The bride and bridegroom left the hall, and Susan and Sumitra moved to another room with the rest of the guests to enjoy a good meal before they left. Slowly people began to drift away from the Hindu Centre.

Ganesha had certainly answered their prayers. It had been a most enjoyable and successful occasion, the sun had shone, and everything had gone without a hitch.

LIFE GOES ON

Kamala left with her new husband for his home in London on the same day, but after a week or so she would be coming back to visit her family for a few days. Often a bride finds her new life rather strange at first, and this custom gives her the chance to see her family without everyone thinking that she is running home to mother.

Even if she did not manage to come home then, she could still look forward to seeing her family in the autumn at the festival of Nava Ratri, and that was only five or six months away. It was an old custom that brides came home at least once a year for this festival, and Kamala would be sure to come home if she were able to. After all, she was still part of the family, and she would be expected to join them at Nava Ratri if she could.

There we have to leave the Patel family. We have spent the best part of a year with them. During that time Krishna and Sumitra have settled in to a new school, and made friends with Peter and Susan; a Hindu Centre has been opened in their town, with the result that the Hindus can worship in their own way in the Prayer Hall in the evenings, and it is much easier to celebrate the festivals.

Deepak was born in the autumn, and Dadaji died soon after at the age of seventy-two years. But winter gave way to spring and soon it was time for the festival of Holi. No sooner had they recovered from these festivities than it was necessary to make preparations for Kamala's wedding.

And so the cycle of life and death and the cycle of the seasons go on. If you are a Hindu, you believe that God is everywhere and in everything. So as you go about your daily life, you show respect to all the people you meet, and to all living beings; indeed there is something of God in all human beings, whoever they may be, whatever their race, religion, or customs.

This prayer sums up what many Hindus believe:

May our bodies be your home, and may everything we enjoy be an offering to you:
May our every word be a hymn to you, our every act your adoration, our every step a pilgrimage to your shrine;
May we see the whole world as lighted by your light, and may we know you as our very own self.

Om, Shanti, Shanti, Shanti.

LIST OF HINDU FESTIVALS

Shiva Ratri, the festival in honour of the great Shiva. Worshippers spend most of the day and night singing his praises.
Birthday of Shri Ramakrishna, a Hindu saint of the nineteenth century.
Holi, the festival of spring.
Ram Naumi, the birthday of Lord Rama.
Raksha Bandhan, a festival of friendship.
Janam Ashtami, the birthday of Lord Krishna.
Ganesha Chaturthi, the festival in honour of Ganesha, the elephant-headed god.
Nava Ratri, the festival of Durga the Divine Mother.
Dussehra, which marks the end of *Nava Ratri* and celebrates the victory of Rama over the demon-king Ravana.
Diwali, the New Year festival of lights.

Although this is not a complete list, these are the main festivals celebrated by Hindus in Britain. An annual calendar of religious festivals is prepared at the R.E. Centre, West London Institute of Higher Education, for the S H A P Working Party and can be obtained from the Community Relations Commission, 15–16 Bedford Street, London WC2E 9HX.